I SEE YOU!

Sawubona!
Y. B. Zungu
_2022_

Books of Poetry by Y.B. Taylor

"Keeping It Real! A Book of Poetry and No Excuses" ©2015
ISBN 978-1-5027-9407-9

"Out of Bounds in an Inbound World" ©2014
ISBN 978-1-4918-4651-3

"Journeys of Freedom" ©2011
ISBN 978-1-4634-2815-0

"What I Know…Poems of Life" ©2009
ISBN 978-1-4389-7007-3

I SEE YOU!

POEMS OF AWARENESS, EMPOWERMENT, AND INSPIRATION

Y.B. TAYLOR

To ebony kings and queens for which
the struggle continues.

AWARENESS*, the ability to directly know and perceive, to feel, or to be of events. More broadly, it is the state or quality of being conscious of something.

EMPOWERMENT* refers to measures designed to increase the degree of autonomy and self-determination in people and in communities in order to enable them to represent their interests in a responsible and self-determined way, acting on their own authority. Empowerment, as action, refers both to the process of self-empowerment and to professional support of people, which enables them to overcome their sense of powerlessness and lack of influence, and to recognize and use their resources.

INSPIRATION* or **INSPIRE** may refer to:
- Artistic inspiration, sudden creativity in artistic production
- Biblical inspiration, the doctrine in Judeo-Christian theology concerned with the divine origin of the Bible
- Creative inspiration, sudden creativity when a new invention is created
- Inhalation, the movement of air into the lungs, breathing in

*As defined by Wikipedia

CONTENTS

FOREWORD

"I'm back by popular demand. I did not come to play...
I came to slay."

"Formation" – Beyonce

FIRST THINGS FIRST (2YBT):

> *If ever you thirst for a mind blowing verse – Let me exclaim*
> *and remember her name – I'll shout it out loud so all may*
> *know it – Y.B. Taylor is the most bomb poet!"*

Remarkable how love can awaken your inner poet. I am so in love with the soul stirring, consciousness raising artistry of the talented Y.B. Taylor. I am in awe of the passion and wisdom that pour from each page and the proliferation of her work. She has gifted the universe with five powerful volumes of verse and I have savored every one. Her latest literary offering, "I SEE YOU!" is another treasure, a celebration of African American achievement, a love song to the Motherland, a scintillating commentary on our cultural and political landscape.

Fans will rejoice that she is as bold, savvy and sassy as ever, tuned in and fired up! "I SEE YOU!" delivers messages of praise as in AMERICAN ROYALS and TO SIR WITH LOVE, as well as warnings to read BETWEEN THE LINES and beware, A STORM'S A COMING! She can see beauty and derive meaning from routine occurrences, like a refreshing rain in CLEANSED, the BLESSINGS of a new day, and even the act of breathing in NAMASTE! Yet, her keen eyes are focused laser-like on serious issues and turbulent events that threaten our families and our freedoms. She declares, I WILL NOT STAND for being shot down, shut down or held down.

There is seemingly no terrain where she dare not tread. The potent poems in this book address topics as diverse as the **Legacy Of**

President Obama in YOU AIN'T SEEN NOTHING YET!, the cries of *Make America Great Again,* and the DOUBLE STANCE for an unnamed Olympic swimmer turned national embarrassment. We get a double serving of spice in GINGER BREDS as she combines notes on Beyonce's formidable performance at the Super Bowl and Jada Pinkett Smith's courageous calling out #oscarssowhite. Y.B. Taylor tells it like it is, how it was, and the way it ought to be!

I have always believed the best writing accomplishes several tasks. It commands your attention, evokes strong feeling, compels you to think, and inspires you to act. Y.B. Taylor excels in every regard. She garners your rapt attention and respect when she refrains, AIN'T GOT TIME FOR CRAZY! She proceeds to explain "crazy as in lacking common sense or choosing not to use it," then lays out what a real woman wants. You feel the tender emotion, love and pride in the tribute to BROWN SUGAR (Queen Sisters). Your mind cannot help but ponder the ignorance, evil, and injustices of those who act as though they are LICENSED TO HATE! When she urges readers to, *"rise and meet your potential"* in the poem, BE MORE, you will want to stand and cheer.

Reading Y.B. Taylor's poetry evokes a multi-sensory experience. You almost smell the "oh-so sweet rich fertilized life-giving soil" of the Motherland in I SEE MYSELF. It is easy to visualize the poignant Gordon Parks photos in IMAGERY from the VMFA exhibit. Surely, I could hear the choir and congregation singing spirituals in TAKE ME TO CHURCHA! Page after page, the rhythm of her writing, the syncopation of the verse bring to mind tribal drumbeats and village elders chanting, *"yes, go, tell them my child."* All of these poems speak to me, move me, leave an impression on my heart. It would be hard to pick a favorite. However I find most endearing the hope and promise expressed in NOT OF YOU. We don't have to be like each other to respect each other. The notion that "progress can only be made with everybody's story," is something we should all champion.

I applaud my cousin's ability to paint a picture and tell a story with her writing. She has always been an engaging wordsmith. From her days as a columnist with our high school newspaper to her current role as a conduit of the family's archivist, her mother – my Aunt Muriel, she is always enlightening and entertaining. Our extended family benefits from the research and we enjoy the anecdotes passed down through generations. Writing is her joy and a gift that she generously shares. My cousin accompanied me and other family and friends on a European trip to celebrate my (milestone) birthday. Shortly after our return, Y.B. presented me with a book that she put together documenting all our adventures in sightseeing, excursions, theater, nightclubs, shopping and dining. It is something I will always cherish.

MY "BREAKING NEWS" TIPS: *Buy this book, read it, and gift the collection to friends and family. Share these poems, read them out loud in book clubs, classrooms, reunions and other gatherings. These poems are instructive and uplifting. They speak to significant ties that bind us; they offer important lessons.*

SAWUBONA! Y. B. Taylor, "I See **YOU**!" I see your brilliance, your truth, your fearlessness, your heart. Most importantly, you have given us enthralling poetry in which we can see ourselves and smile, feeling proud, recognized and appreciated. Thank you!

Sabrina Squire
TV News Anchor
Multi Emmy Award Winner
VCU Virginia Communications Hall Of Fame

ACKNOWLEDGMENTS

Isn't it funny how a minor decision can have a major impact?

Several of the prompts for the poetry in this book were inspired as a result of my own absentmindedness. I had forgotten I had registered for *Busting Through the Bucket List,* a workshop facilitated by Marsha Snead Williams-Cawley.

Before attending the workshop, I had decided I needed to SMILE more. (*I have never been that person who smiles for no apparent reason while going about her daily life. It is not that I am unhappy, but walking around with a smile plastered on my face is not my thing.*) I acknowledge Marsha's aka *The Butterfly Queen's* charisma and effervescent personality, for providing a workshop that left me rejuvenated, empowered, and smiling. Thank you Marsha for facilitating *Busting Through the Bucket List.* **BROWN SUGAR**

I acknowledge my mother who I try to emulate in expressing myself in a lady-like manner. Unfortunately, I am not always successful in achieving that goal. I acknowledge my father, who was known for his unsolicited advising and expressing of self. (*Much to my mother's dismay, I inherited his DNA for that "character trait."*)

I acknowledge my cousin, award-winning news anchor Sabrina Squire, one of my staunchest supporters, for writing the Foreword for this book. Sabrina, your charitable words literally scared me. Upon receiving and reading your Foreword, I started wondering whether my poetry actually lived up to all the accolades you were bestowing, i.e., was I worthy? Thank you cuz for your vote of confidence and continuous support! Love you much... Time for another girls trip. **FAMILY!**

I acknowledge being "called out," by my husband, for not presenting more positive poems elevating and celebrating our kings. **TO SIR, WITH LOVE** is dedicated to the black men in and out of my life, past and present... men of integrity, love, family-first values, and intelligence, including but not limited to my father, my husband, my paternal grandfather[1], my godfather, my many, many male relatives (I dare not name individuals for fear of inadvertently omitting some), and to my workout partners (regular and part-time), as well as Darryl Ellis of DNA Fitness, who writes prolifically on social media. It was one of his thought provoking POSTS that prompted me to "weigh-in" with **GINGER BREDS.** *Your FRIENDS and FOLLOWERS await your first book!*

I acknowledge Challie (AFF-VCC) for her nod of approval and for not giving up when I was hesitant to try Hot Vinyasa Yoga. I may not be one of the most consistent and dedicated participants, but I always leave class feeling composed, relaxed and centered. **NAMASTE!**

I acknowledge Willis "Tracee" Davis III (1949-2015); "Rest in Peace!" Thank you for allowing me to hover over your shoulders and ask incessant questions when you were creating beautiful graphic art on the computer. Because of Tracee's encouragement and assurance that I have *skillz*, I had the confidence to design the cover for this, my fifth literary child. Tracee, you have not been forgotten. **NOT OF YOU!**

Wishing to see the good in people and desiring the disenfranchised to look within themselves and discover their own self-worth and strength, I acknowledge finding inspiration in Jesse Williams' acceptance speech at the 2016 BET Awards. **BE MORE!**

Lastly and humbly, I acknowledge my eternal gratitude to and faith in God for blessing me with the desire and gift to write.

INTRODUCTION

"He who does not know can know from learning."

NEA ONNIM NO SUA A. OHU
Adinkra symbol of "knowledge,
life-long education and continued
quest for knowledge"

DISCLAIMER: *Because I am protective of my literary "children," all editing is by yours truly. I apologize, in advance, and accept all responsibility for misspelled words, errors in punctuation, word use, page alignment, etc.*

Introducing my "fifth literary child," *I SEE YOU! Poems of Awareness, Empowerment, and Inspiration*. This "child" contains poems that will entertain, inspire, empower, provoke, and educate! *I SEE YOU!,* like *Keeping It Real,* has Endnotes and Appendices, for educating and teaching.

I challenged myself to write poetry that would make others as well as me **S-M-I-L-E**! Both, my intent and resolve, were tested by multiple events occurring in 2016. Unfortunately, or fortunately, depending on your perspective, I composed many reactionary poems. During the summer, America was rocked with news of back-to-back police shootings of two more young African American males.[2] Days later, five Dallas, Texas, police officers were shot and killed.[3] **A STORM'S A-COMING!** A month later, the celebratory spirit of the Olympic games was tarnished by actions of U.S. Olympic swimmers. **DOUBLE STANCE** Towards the end of the year, the outcome of the Presidential elections provoked massive rallies, unrest, protests, and racially-motivated assaults and killings across America. **ON HIGH ALERT!**

While I may be smiling more, my smiles do not always denote happiness; sometimes a smile will be an outward display of relief of having captured and conveyed the essence of my thoughts in a poem. Going forth, where possible, I will attempt to honor my challenge by inserting positive perspectives and/or spins regardless of situations or outcomes.

With this book, I have come to a realization…

- ❖ I wish to be recognized as an educator, though I could never be in a classroom on a daily basis.
- ❖ I wish to be recognized as an instigator of thought, though I do not wish to debate.
- ❖ I wish to be recognized as a student of history, though I never enjoyed history classes.
- ❖ I wish to be recognized as someone somewhat knowledgeable about current events; that's it… there is no THOUGH!

Through my poetry, I hope to enlighten those who have not walked the path of being a minority within a minority in America, a country I embrace as my own, but a country that does not always reciprocate my embrace or the embrace of those similar to me, a country divided. **LICENSED TO HATE!**

Lastly, one of the most difficult tasks – for me – in constructing books of poetry is determining the sequence of the poems. The poems contained in **"I SEE YOU!"** have been printed alphabetically by their titles.

I could claim insight
I could claim knowledge
I claim neither
I claim what I am…
A black woman surviving

Through poetic expression
Of her truths, beliefs
Perspectives and thoughts
No couldas,
No wouldas,
No shouldas
Just truths, dreams, beliefs,
Perspectives, and thoughts!

INTRODUCING... **I SEE YOU!**

POEMS OF AWARENESS, EMPOWERMENT, AND INSPIRATION

"Bad spirits fill empty spaces."

Spoken by character **Jules**
"3 Days to Kill" (2014)

A STORM'S A-COMING!

Storm clouds gather

Enveloping the world

The sun shines

But, a storm's a-coming!

Hate, indifference magnified

Fueling instabilities of diseased minds

Radicals and radical wannabes

Domestic and foreign

Wreak havoc with reckless abandon

Chain reactions of evil and civil unrest

A storm's a-coming!

World citizens fear armaments of destruction

Tire of bigoted oppression

Dread things will get worst before they get better

Young watch and learn bad behaviors from old

A storm's a-coming!

Body cams, phones and social media
Witness the criminal, insane, inane
And incomprehensible
Proliferating an abundance of hashtags

#BlackLivesMatter
#HandsUpDontShoot
#ICantBreathe
#ParisAttacks
#NiceAttack
#BacktheBlue
#AllLivesMatter
#EnoughIsEnough

AIN'T GOT TIME FOR CRAZY!

Contrary to what many believe

I ain't[4] got time for crazy!

Not a holler-back or holler-at girl

Intrusion into my periphery

With whistles and innuendos

Is unwelcomed

Yes, I am short

But, 'Shorty' **is not** my name

I am not **yo' baby**

Nor am I **yo' mama**

I know my father

You are not he

I know my children

You are not one of them

I am not Miss Thang or Sweet Thing

I am not stuck up

I simply choose not to respond

Cause…

I ain't got time for crazy!

Not crazy as in… mentally challenged

But crazy ~ as in…

No respect for yourself

And… no respect for others

Crazy – as in…

Lacking common sense

Or… **choosing** not to use it

You see…

Contrary to what many believe

Real women don't have time for crazy

Real women are not

Holler-back or holler-at girls

Intrusion into a real woman's periphery

With whistles and innuendos

Is unwelcomed

A real woman is a queen

Desirous of a real king

Not a gangster wannabe

Raised middle class

4

Or a gangster pressured to be
  Because of poverty

A real woman is a queen
  Seeking a real king
  Respectful of queens
  Regardless of age
  Regardless of color
  Regardless of girth

A real woman is a queen
  Seeking a real king
  Knowledgeable and proud
  Of his own self worth

Once monarchs,
  Possessing power
Once kings and queens,
  Honoring family…
  Our greatest treasure
Once preeminent scholars
  Possessing infinite knowledge
  Leading the world in the sciences
Once spiritual and one with the land…
  Revering elders
  The backbone of their culture

Unfortunately, today many do **do** crazy
Not crazy as in…
  Mentally challenged

But crazy ~ as in…

    No respect for self

Crazy – as in…

    No respect for others

Crazy ~ as in…

    Lacking common sense

    Or **choosing** not to use it

So!...

When I do not respond

Know your intrusion into my periphery

With whistles and innuendos

Is unwelcomed

Regardless of age

Color, profession, or wealth

There's no expiration on crazy

And…

I

ain't

got

time

for

crazy!

"You were born a queen, it's in your DNA."

Unknown

AMERICAN ROYALS

Stately

Approachable

Educated

Natural beauties

Of exceptional DNA

Not misstepping

Nor bringing shame

    While millions watch

They come into their own

    Becoming women

    Becoming queens

    In a paparazzi

    Social media world

Poised… sure

    Not impulsive

Not affluenza teens

    Because of who and where they are

Truly meritorious

They are American royals

They are … **<u>my</u>** President's daughters[5]

BE MORE

Be more than beautiful

    Be the face of a proud race

Be more than sculpted arms and abs

    Be a body standing strong with others

Be more than a user of words

    Be a speaker for equality and justice

Be more than a brand wearer

    Be adorned with integrity and pride

Speak truth

    Use words a child can hear and understand

    Words elders can readily praise

    Don't whitewash

    Don't throw shade[6]

Speak truth

    Truth is the light…

    Let it shine on public servant drive-bys

    Let it shine on divisive politicos

Let it shine on systematic bigotry

Let it shine on disparity in education

Let it shine on inequality in housing

Let it shine on inconsistencies in employment

Let it shine on disproportionate incomes

Let it shine on attitudes

    Them vs. Us

    He vs. She

It is time to step up

    Not remain seated[7]

It is time to take action

    By any means necessary![8]

Words with action... not empty promises

    If I could, I would, but... *Excuses!*[9]

Be more...

    Meet your potential

    Coulda, shoulda, woulda, but didn't

Be more...

    Don't get worn and used

Be more...

    Rise!

Inspired by Jesse Williams' speech
2016 BET Awards
[Appendix B – Full transcript]

BETWEEN THE LINES

Many truths told in jest

Ploys to mislead and beguile

Politicians, like everyday people

Insult, camouflage with smiles

What and how they speak **to** you

    Of another's plight

Is what and how they speak **of** you

    When you are not in sight

Be aware and learn to read between the lines!

BLESSINGS

Poised, skin glistening

    Supple, soft, and brown

Steady pelts of rain excite

    Gracing curves

    Hugging legs

    Caressing mounds

With eyes closed

    Green lushness is envisioned

    Surrounding a shallow pool

    Its depths unperceived

Step into the warming cool

    Shiver and anticipate

    A promise of purification

Look skyward between palms of shade

    Catch rays of sun

While blue skies beckon you to ride

Capacious puffs of white

Floating one horizon to another

Raise arms

Grasp hovering dewdrops

That embrace deflecting sunrays

And create vibrant rainbows

With promises of treasures

At their arc's end

Be thankful for yet another day of blessings

BLUE THUNDER

A solitary wave

    Silently glides over sand

Erasing slight imprints

    Of a walker's strides

Not too far in the distance

    Deep, blue-green, translucent waters

    Churn and froth

    Joining in force

    Prepping a wall of power

    Shape-shifting and unpredictable

    Thunderously crashing and assaulting

    Never-ending, rolling and roaring

Seductive sprays

    Refract and disperse sunlight

Seductive sprays

    Capable of crushing coral

    Shells, lava rock, stone and more!

    Creating sandy beaches

    Pink, red, black, and white

Multi-hued like walkers who stride

Sandy beaches readying themselves

    For solitary rolling and caressing waves

Sandy beaches readying themselves

    For battalions of thunderous assaulting waves

Waves erasing slight imprints

    Of walkers' strides

On immense and inviting sandy shores

Inspired by
Ke'e Beach, Nā Pali Coast
Kauai, Hawaii

"The blacker the berry, the sweeter the juice."

African American proverb

BROWN SUGAR

Queen sisters, sister queens

Products and by-products of Mother Africa

Celebrate sweetness of our brown sugar

Sweetened, raw, unprocessed and natural

Sugar cane, yam, African bee honey sweet

Mother Land indigenous fruits

Yellow-brown nectar… more valuable than gold

Coveted by many

A treasure worth protecting

Resplendent in taste

Flavor and texture

Individually

Collectively

Brown sugar queens heighten desires

Contribute to textures of conversations

Sometimes crystallizing hard-candy facts

Not fudging truth for uninitiated

Queen sisters, sister queens
Celebrate sweetness of our brown sugar
Caramelizing saltiness and acidity of many

Queen sisters, sister queens
Stretch the sweetness of our honey-brown sugar
Lowering chill and freezing-out some
While raising boiling points of others

Queen sisters, sister queens
Do not allow sweetness of our brown sugar
Belie power we possess

Know properties of our sweetness
Mixed in varying concentrations
 Define softness
 Define tenderness
 Define rigidity
 Define toughness

Queen sisters, sister queens
Products and by-products of Mother Africa
Celebrate sweetness of our brown sugar

CLEANSED

How soothing,

How cleansing,

Refreshing,

Releasing,

    A hard and steady rain

In light of day,

In dark of night,

    Washing away dust,

    Washing away trash,

    Bringing life to plants,

    Bringing life to grass,

    Bringing life to barren soil

How soothing,

How cleansing,

Refreshing,

Releasing,

    A hard and steady rain

If only, a hard and steady rain

Were all it took

    To cleanse

    To refresh

    To release

    Wrongs of the world

    Failures of man

If only, a hard and steady rain

    Could wash

    Refresh

    Release

Soil from our minds

Soil from our mouths

Soil from our thoughts

    Refreshing

    Releasing anew

Cleansed attitudes of life

*"Fairness is an across-the-board requirement for all our
interactions with each other… Fairness treats
everybody the same."*

Barbara C. Jordan (1936-1996)
*First African American elected
to the Texas Senate after
Reconstruction; first southern
black female elected to the U.S.
House of Representatives, and
first African American woman
to deliver the keynote address at
a Democratic Nat'l Convention*

DOUBLE STANCE

"Boys will be boys," except…

When they are men

Ad nauseam and in the news!

Read and hear of…

Aggressive, boorish, illegal behavior

Even an international incident

By a not-so-young male[10]

Who happened to be white

But, "boys will be boys"

Oft times destruction of property

Unjustified, but qualified

Because "they were bored"

And, "boys will be boys"

Assault, battery
    Even sexual misconduct[11]
    Deemed negligible

Abbreviated sentences
    Suspension of time
    Because futures were at hand
And, "boys will be boys"

Yet, a young boy dies
    For doing what young boys do
    … Play with toy guns[12]

A young boy dies
    For doing what young boys do
    … Play in abandoned buildings[13]

A young boy dies
    For doing what many do everyday
    … Accidently bump a stranger[14]

A young boy dies
    For doing what young boys should not do
    … Menace police with a knife[15]
    But, mental illness was a factor

But, these "boys could not be boys"
    And will never be men
    Because these boys were not white

These boys were black,

    Each seen as man-child

    Age nor size a factor

    Disposable as trash

These boys were...

    Perceived hulking

    Deemed men

    Deemed threatening

    Deemed capable of monstrous deeds

    Deemed not "boys being boys"

Whether culpable or innocent

    Treating men as boys

    'Cause "boys will be boys"

    Must come to an end

Whether culpable or innocent

    Treating boys as men

    'Cause...

    There is no justifiable 'cause

Double stance needs to end!

Fannie Lou Hamer (1917-1977)
American voting rights activist,
civil rights leader, and
philanthropist

ENCRYPTED EPIDEMIC

Cryptograms around us

Inscribed, forecasting fate

Contaminants spewed daily

Containing microcosms of hate

An epidemic brewing

    Calm before the storm

Must hunker down

Secure position

Prepare for intent of harm

The prognosis unsettling

Solutions imprecise

Diagnosis essential

For survival, for life

No placebos, no BAND-AID®

    No drugs from FDA

Can suppress the inflammation

Of hate and malice, the mainstay

Like the scarecrow and the tin man
Requiring new thoughts and heart
Like the cowardly lion
Finding courage for a new start

We must decrypt the "intelligence"
And learn to read the signs
Become skilled as our elders
Leaving no one behind

Parents always warned
Be careful the company you keep
Wash and don't ingest
After shaking hands when you meet

From years of internalization
There is no way to know
The sores that have been harbored
Masked and festering below

Externally, there may be smiling
But, they are not your friend
May we all survive this epidemic
And breathe fresh air again

Langston Hughes (1902-1967)
American poet, social activist,
novelist, playwright, and
columnist

FAMILY

Respecting and celebrating family

> Family of blood

> Family of love

> Family of friends

Bonds and connections

> Years in formation

> Outlasting sands of time

Bonds newly made

> With much in common

> Like we've known one another

> For all time

Blood, often taken for granted

> Friends sometimes closer

Family sometimes "trying"

> Making you wonder,

> "Why must this be so difficult?"

But blood is thicker than water

> And, family is forever

"Fear is a disease that eats away at logic and makes man inhuman."

Marian Anderson (1897-1993)
American contralto; one of the most celebrated singers of 20th century; first African American to perform with New York Metropolitan Opera

FEAR

For no other reason than melanin

Fear has nestled

In the minds of those

Not comprehending diversity

For no other reason than religion

Fear has burrowed a hole

In the hearts of those

Disdaining diversity

For no other reason than sexual orientation

Fear has dug its talons

Into the subconscious of those

Disparaging diversity

For no other reason than culture

Fear has tunneled into the souls of those

Vilifying diversity

For no other reason than ignorance

Fear of non-English speech

Has closed the ears of those

Mocking diversity

Alarmed by diversity

    Hard-hearted fear-mongers

    Think themselves formidable

    Think themselves dominant

    Think themselves superior

Their fear based tactics

    Exaggeration and repetitious lies

    Exposing their insecurities

Because they are narrow-minded

    And do not wish

    To comprehend diversity

*"I don't know what the future may hold, but I know
who holds the future."*

Ralph Abernathy (1926-1990)
*Leader of Civil Rights
Movement, a minister, and
King's closest friend*

GINGER BREDS

Wake up America!

Don't choose to SNOOZE!

Sun signs rise

And, Virgos[16] roar

Detail-oriented

Born to serve

Two ginger breds

Couture styled

Well coiffed

Deep pocketed

Connected

Lead the charge

Exercising Freedom of Speech

Putting on blast two-years

"White only" Oscars[17]

Network TV scrambles

While Super Bowl video[18] frazzles

With reminders of Katrina

And, "Black Lives Matter"

A child dances

Armed police stand

Signage displays, "Don't Shoot!"

Opponents cry "foul!"

How dare ginger breds overstep

    Roles of entertaining

How dare ginger breds take a stand

    Galvanizing conscious thought

How dare ginger breds

    Couture styled

    Well coiffed

    Deep pocketed

    Connected

Upset Norman Rockwell's America

How dare they make us care?

Cries of "Make America great again"

Coded ~ "Put them in their place!"

    Falls on deaf ears

Because ginger breds dared to risk

    Falling from favor

By exercising Freedom of Speech

"The greatest glory in living lies not in never failing, but in rising every time we fall."

Nelson Mandela (1918-2013)
South African anti-apartheid revolutionary, lawyer, politician, and philanthropist; President of South Africa after 27-years imprisonment

GOT MY SIX

Paranoia, not my claim

    Family and friends have my six[19]

Societal norms clearly the blame

    Family and friends have my six

Never taking chances

    Assuming zilch

Type A – I don't proclaim

But observations for preservation

    And, family and friends have my six

A look of disdain

    …or even worst

    No longer seems to suffice

Physical presence insufficient

    Most resort to deadly devices

Thrilled, ecstatic and overjoyed

My confrontations are few

Thrilled, ecstatic and overjoyed

With family and friends of every hue

And...

Family and friends have my six!

GRAY MATTER MATTERS

The struggle continues

The work, never done

Advancements attained

There's more to move on

No time to step back

Resting on laurels

No time to slack off

Beg or borrow

The challenge remains

To continue the fight

Slacking begets weakness

Losing sight of what's right

Nothing is given
Without something in return
Bad and wrong choices
"Should be" lessons learned

Not getting called
On wrongs done
Doesn't mean wrongs forgotten
The works just begun

Education, academics
Not athletics, nor sports
Should place first
As top priority choice

Strengthening gray matter
Of all girls and boys
Sports and athletics
Should be tools to enjoy

With sports, a simple fall
Can decimate a career
While strengthened and conditioned brains
Will sustain for years

Those in top offices
May resemble wimps
But those in top offices
Are the true pimps!

Education, academics

A priority exist

Damaged bones, torn muscles

Dangerous precipices

Ascend, ascend

    To attainable heights

        Because gray matter matters!

I APOLOGIZE

I apologize…

Not for myself

    But for those who taunt

Darker-skin sisters [and brothers]

    But, mostly sisters

Imposing their own self-hatred

Ignorance and lack of esteem

Unsure of themselves

They find solace in deprecating

Extraordinary beauty of ebony skin

And yet,

An ebony skin brother may get a 'pass'

Or may decide to 'pass'

On a like-skin sister

I apologize…

Not for myself

But, for those who ridicule

Darker-skin sisters [and brothers]

But, mostly sisters

Making them feel

Less woman [less man], less desirable

And yet,

An ebony skin brother will get a 'pass'

Or may decide to 'pass'

On a like-skin sister

I apologize…

Not for myself

But, for the snubs and exclusions[20]

Because ebony beauty

Was not [is not] recognized

For what it is… pure and undiluted

How is it

Others see ebony beauty

But [we] do not

Why is it

[We] interject and qualify the ebony beauty

Of darker-skin sisters [and brothers]

But, mostly sisters

Stating "For a dark-skin, …"

I apologize…

Not for myself

    But, for those unlike me

    Who say, have said

    Do, have done

    Imply, have implied anything

Making you… my ebony-skin sisters [and brothers]

    But, mostly sisters

Feel any less than what you are…

                B-E-A-U-T-I-F-U-L!

I SEE MYSELF

I see myself a Nubian beauty

Black as coal

Like deepest, darkest Congo of Tarzan Africa

Motherland... Cradle of civilization

I see myself broad of nose

Inhaling oh-so sweet rich fertilized life-giving soil

Cleansing nasal passages of urbanization

I see myself wide of childbearing hips

Birthing kings, queens, scholars

Exuding confidence in regality

Crown high, chest proud... not pompous

I see myself one of a people

Masters and mistresses of stars and seas

Builders of obelisks and pyramids

Potion discerners of herbs and plants

Textile creators of color and beauty

I see myself a warrior

    Fighting for just-us justice

    Combating negative perceptions

    Upholding family values

    Encouraging standards in self

I see myself one of many

    Textile creators of color and beauty

    Potion discerners of herbs and plants

    Builders of obelisks and pyramids

    Masters and mistresses of stars and seas

I see myself one of a people

    Crown high, chest proud… not pompous

    Exuding confidence in regality

    Birthing kings, queens, scholars

    I see myself wide of childbearing hips

Cleansed nasal passages of urbanization

    Inhaling oh-so sweet rich fertilized life-giving soil

    I see myself broad of nose

Motherland… Cradle of civilization

    Like deepest, darkest Congo of Tarzan Africa

    Black as coal

I see myself a Nubian beauty[21]

Malcolm X (1925-1965)
Born Malcolm Little, also known as el-Hajj Malik el-Shabazz, was African American minister of the Nation of Islam and human rights activist

I WILL NOT STAND

Blindfolded

Hands bound

Back against the wall

I will not stand

To be shot down

Blinded by lies

Hands tied

Backed against the wall

I will not stand

For being shut down

Eyes focused

Hands reaching

Knocking down walls

I will not stand

For being held down

Eyes engaged
Hands employed
Breaking through walls
I will not stand
For being backed down

Eyes on the prize
Hands clenched
Walls broken
I will not stand
For being talked down

I will stand for justice
I will stand for equality
I will stand for respect
Not just "out of respect"

I will take a stand
To stand
I will take a stand
To sit
I will take a stand
To kneel[22]

I will take a stand
For inalienable rights
That are mine
As an American
Born and raised
To stand

To sit

To kneel

To raise a fist[23]

To protest injustices

To protest inequality

To protest disrespect

To protest oppression

It is my inalienable right

To exercise my right

To take a stand!

IMAGERY

A photo speaks…

Emits no sound

But, listen…

Hear raw emotions[24]

Above pain and suffering

Hear dignity and integrity

Gelatin silver print[25] displays

Primarily black and white

Heightening visual senses

Hear what eyes perceive

Years of poverty

Years of discrimination

Years of indignation

Years of segregation

A photo speaks...

Listen for a visual of hope

A visual of progress

A visual of humanity

A visual of equality

A visual of justice

Open closed ears and minds

Listen, as a photo speaks... VOLUMES

Inspired by VMFA exhibit:
Gordon Parks: Back to Fort Scott

LEST WE FORGET

Many denounce history

Saying it belongs in the past

But, how do we progress in time

If history we do not grasp

Lest we forget…

History is not retractable

It can't be lied away

Excuses for behaviors then

Dry rot, wear thin, and fray

Lest we forget…

Slavery, Jim Crow, the Holocaust

Now decades and scores away

Can come again in different forms

When from history we decide to stray

Lest we forget…

History tends to teach
The paths we must avoid
Alienation, discrimination
Based on discord

Lest we forget…

Have and Have-nots
Will always be at odds
Haves wheeling and dealing
Have-nots… dealt bad cards

Lest we forget…

History… good, bad, and ugly
Is not for the faint of heart
History… good, bad, and ugly
Provides our future's start

LICENSED TO HATE!

My heart bleeds

My eyes tear

    For those who feel *"licensed to hate"*

Entitled to lob

Verbal, physical *"hits"*

    Against those unlike themselves

Shouts of *"Make America great **again!**"*

    Translate to *"white is right"*

    All others can *"go back"*

    As in *"to where they came from"*

No remorse, no demarcation

    Towards targets of hate

Brown, yellow, black, red, tan

    Old and young… targets

Refusals of reality

Denials to realization

It is not just <u>we</u> but also *<u>they</u>*

Who are outsiders

Forgetting their family roots

Were transplanted, not indigenous

Generations forgetting they were once

    "The tired, the poor, the huddled masses

    Yearning to breathe free[26]"

Not recognizing

Native Americans alone

Corralled and small-poxed

Have the right to indignation

    Numbers brutalized

    Lands confiscated

    Tribes annihilated

    Placed on reservations

        For "their own good"

Too few in number to retaliate

    A "Trail of Tears"[27]

When will entitled *"licensed to hate"*

Realize their bile

Has sickened and killed

Still sickens and kills

The spirit of America

    Treasured by the majority

    Brown, yellow, black, red, tan

    And yes, white

Who will galvanize, sending those *"licensed to hate"*

Back to where they came from

"Keeping America Great!"

"And that is life."

Paul Laurence Dunbar (1872-1906)
American poet, novelist, and
playwright of late 19th century
and early 20th centuries

MISSION ACCOMPLISHED

Perfection sought

But remains unclaimed

Unlike nature

Where imperfections and flaws

Exist as beautifully perfect

For man and wo-man

There is no perfection

Always but(s), if(s), or(s)

And and(s)

Swap words

Use Thesaurus

Edit, tweak to meet intent

Some rhyme, no rhyme

And many mini tales of…

Life's encounters

Life's observations

Life's perspectives

Pause… comma

Extension of thought… semi colon

Unfinished thought… ellipsis

Emphasis of thought… *italicize*, **bold**

There's always more… period

Alice Walker (1944-)
American author, National Book Award recipient, Pulitzer Prize winner for fiction, and activist

MOTHER LODE

Mothers of this world

Walk with dignity

Heads high

Shoulders unbowed

Classic beauties

Mothers of this world

Threadbare worn

Step bare of foot

Yet...

Mothers of this world

Nurture

Provide food when there is little

Shelter where there is none

Protect in face of danger

So strong

So powerful

So triumphant

Mothers of this world

So superior in strength

Mere addition to the mundane

Fortifies, enriches and empowers

Earth Mothers of Mother Land

Mother Africa

Mother Goddess of Mother Earth

Forgotten Mother Tongue

Observed Mother Nature

Survived Mother Ship

Used Mother Wit

With sisters Mother Craft and Mother Hen

And created Mothers Superior

MY POWER COMES

My power comes

    Not from strength and conditioning

    Or my resolve to maintain good health

My power comes from knowing and desiring

    To better understand myself

A self who wants to know

    Who, what, when and where

A self who wants to know

    Why and how

A self who values lessons learned

    Because with knowledge comes my power

Maya Angelou (1926-2014)
American poet, memoirist,
civil rights activist, actress

NAMASTE!

Eyes closed

Breathing composed

A zone of serenity sought…

Woosah!

Mind cleared of problems

If not but for this moment

I am released

Inhale – and – hold…

Woosah!

Body oxygenated

Internal heat developing

Chakra![28]

Reposed or lotus

Thoughts are centered

Exhale slow – count – to – ten …

Woosah!

Rhythm maintained
Energy building
Ujjayi[29] breaths
Victorious
Calming
Balancing…

Woosah!

Staying present
I am aware of self
My practice grounded
Vinyasa[30] strong
Feeling vitality of life force
Coursing throughout…

Woosah!

Body transcends
Embracing inner peace
Peace with self
Peace of being
Happiness with who I am…

Woosah!

Toxins cleared
Mind cleared

If not but for this moment

Savasana![31]

Eyes closed
Breathing composed
I am released
Serenity achieved

Namaste![32]

NO LESS A SLAVE

Had I been born a slave
What would have been my plight?
Assuredly, to have been favored
But, still propertied, a house slave's life

Fair enough to be in charge
Of those propertied like me
Yet dark enough to daily toil
Within on bended knee

Massa would have "loved" me
The missus would have detest
Children born and kin to hers
Knowing better than to protest

Behind closed doors
I'd have run the house
As second in command
Making use of my *"forbidden fruit"*
To forward my escape plan

My freedoms to come
My freedoms to go
    More liberal than those of the fields
But, still papered and propertied
    Away, I yearned to steal

Shackled or shackle-free
    I'd been no less a slave!

NOT OF YOU!

I may not be of you, but...

    I am with you

I need not be like you,

    To respect you

I may not fully comprehend you, but...

    I am willing to try

Who you choose to love

    It's not for me to pry

How you choose to worship

    Can be different from my way

How you dress and wear your hair

    Quite differently from me, but...

Differences offer opportunities

    To learn others culturally

I respect your right to live your life

    Exactly as you choose

As I have same expectations of you for me

    There is nothing here to loose

Some may find change difficult

Resisting acceptance and growth

Preferring to remain stagnant, and…

Antiquated in thought

Change is inevitable

Acceptance not mandatory, but…

Progress can only be made

With everybody's story

ON HIGH ALERT!
(THERE WILL BE NO GOING BACK)

Say what you want

You can even be detached

But, we[34] are here to stay

There will be no going back

Try rolling back legislation

Denying privileges and rights[35]

But, we are telling you now

There will be no going back

Try to ignore us

Like we do not exist

Or fill us with fear

When we persist

Visceral gut-wrenching trauma

Will not be exposed for your pleasure

We have come too far

We have worked too hard

There will be no going back

Ceilings splintered, shattered, broken

Shards of glass pelt and impale

But, we are here, loudly proclaiming

Not cowering from threats of jail

There will be no going back

A monumental edifice

Structured on the nation's Mall[36]

An invitation to come and bear witness

Of history too long on stall

There will be no going back

Your cataract-clouded vision

To realities of the world

And cancerous illusions

Hate-tainted, twisted swirls

Are not our realities

Or a world destined to be

You see...

This is 21st century America

"Land of the Free"

Your illusion of reality

You will never see

Because

There will be no going back

Written post-2016 election

Leontyne Price (1927-)
*Born Mary Violet Leontyne
Price; American soprano, rose to
international acclaim in 1950s
and 1960s; one of first African
Americans to become leading
artist with Metropolitan Opera*

PHENOMENAL!

History distorted

From a white point of view

Years of being told

What we could not do

Not because incapable

But because of hue

We are phenomenal!

No longer given

But taking opportunities,

We prove wrong concepts of…

Ineptness and ability

We are phenomenal!

In every endeavor and every exchange

We prove our acuity

We prove our range

We are phenomenal!

Science and discoveries

Our presence no longer obscure[37]

With sports we break records

We compete, win[38], and endure

Entertainment with awards

In all domains, we reign

Politic with savvy

The White House, we have claimed[39]

We are phenomenal!

Talents mimicked

Aptitudes hidden

Patents stolen

Achievements pirated

BUT... no more

We claim our achievements

We garner our accolades

We flaunt our abilities

BECAUSE...

WE - ARE - PHENOMENAL!

SAWUBONA!

I see you...

> Beyond external shell
>
> I see character
>
> Not extreme
>
> But character far from insignificant

I see you...

> An embodiment of traits
>
> Found in noble beasts
>
> Beasts of the wild
>
> With behaviors we cherish
>
> Behaviors desirable as our own

I see you...

> Commanding
>
> Not demanding attention
>
> A lion, a lioness
>
> Strong and courageous
>
> Protecting
>
> Maintaining pride

Working together

Staying together

I see you...

An elephant, not behemoth

But influencing, sustaining

With ability to resolve and...

Bring about agreement

Noble, gentle, intelligent

Protecting young

Honoring family

I see you with...

Temperament

Ambition

Potential

Essence

I see you...

Committed father

Caring mother

Compassionate elder

Three C's for parenting

Three C's of development

I see you...

Focused to infuse

Ambition

Confidence

Humbleness

Qualities of noble beasts

Sawubona[40]... I see you!

S-M-I-L-E!

Summer's end and a carpet of white butterflies

Scatter, taking flight around my feet

Flowering my path

Were it not for blazing hot sun

Warming my chest, face, bare arms and legs

I'd think them winter snow

Miniature dwarf fountain green grass

Stands tall and bends

Drying, browning and going limp

In anticipation

Of an oncoming cold winter

I sit, face tilted upward with closed eyes

Sun bronzing my already tanned skin

Suppressing emotions and retaining memories

Of visits to other gardens, tropical and lush

Orchids, painted eucalyptus

Volcanic mountain and lava rock

Producing venue specific flora

Lawn mowers and children interrupt my solace

Bringing me back from my revelry of travel

I sit and take pleasure in the innocence of youth

As their brown, tawny, flushed legs run

With 1a to 4c free-flowing and braided locks

Haloing their heads

They have yet to learn the hates of mankind

Enchanted are these moments of ...

Observing the beauty of nature

Memories of travel

Time spent with family and friends

Moments, which bring pleasure to my senses

And, joy to my heart

I smile!

Josephine Baker (1906-1975)
*American-born French jazz and
pop music singer, and actress,
who came to be known in
various circles as the "Black
Pearl," "Bronze Venus," "Jazz
Cleopatra," and even the
"Creole Goddess"*

TAKE ME TO CHURCHA!

Gospels, spirituals

True spoken word

    Take me to churcha!

Feeling the spirit

I am moved and...

Taken to a higher realm

    Take me to churcha!

I rise, I stand

Hands lifted, eyes closed

Not knowing I am standing

The spirit enters

    Take me to churcha!

Old hymns, no hymnals

Back-in-the-day spirituals

Everyone knows the words

    Take me to churcha!

Spoken word, scripture

Cited chapter and verse

Plain talk, real talk

No junk talk, just church talk

    Take me to churcha!

Fed by THE word

Filled by THE spirit

My soul flourishes

    Take me to churcha!

Prayer and praise

    Take me to churcha!

Inspired by visit to
Historic First African Baptist Church[41]
Hilton Head Island, South Carolina

"Here I stand before you – brown. Color of the mountains Colossal as the earth Wrapped so deliciously within my own joy and misery Feathers of my wings paralyzed by the distance of my mind Here I stand before you, the color of the night Frozen by the potential of me." – Lyrics to "Afro Angel"

Will Smith (1968-)
Born Willard Carroll Smith, Jr.; American actor, producer, rapper, and songwriter

TO SIR, WITH LOVE

Black men of whom I am proud

Cherish and call my own

Your presence throughout history, not obscure

Your life force, not cloned

Napoleon tried to emulate

But no Hannibal[42] was he

Desiring an elephant design

For the Triomphe in Pa-ree[43]

Watusi warrior

Jumping Masai

King of Zululand

With small steps

Great heights you achieved

Building empires still grand

Strong ties to past
Strong ties to present
    Honoring ancestors
    Treasuring young
Knowledge stolen, bodies enslaved
And yet, you still live on

DNA survival of Middle Passage
European ails you resist
Slavery, bigotry, systemic discrimination
And yet, you still subsist

Your strength, tenacity, honor and love
    Exudes the king you are
Black as coal or white as cream
    You are my guiding star

TRUTH IS...

This **IS** a "colored" world

    A Crayola® box comprised solely of earth tones

        Hues of brown

        Hues of black

    Multi-dimensional, multi-racial

        Albino, crème fraîche[44]

        Dark chocolate, ebony

Truth is...

    This **IS** a "colored" world

    Unlike a Crayola® box

    There is no purity of white

    No purity of black

    No purity of red or yellow

Truth is...

    This **IS** a "colored" world

    A colored world of pale, fair, and dark skin

Comprised of copious variations between

Pale and fair to dark

Olive skin, ruddy skin

Bronzed, tawny and flushed skin

This **IS** a "colored" world

No purity of white

No purity of black

No purity of red or yellow

This **IS** a "colored" world

Becoming more "colored" with each birth

Mary Anne Radmacher (unknown)
*Author of motivational books
and inspirational quotes, an
artist, and a calligrapher*

WHERE ARE MY PEOPLE?

East, West, North, South

    Where are my people?

Europe, Asia, Aussie-land

    Where are my people?

South America, Antarctica and Arctic pole

    Where are my people?

Traveling, can't help but note

Infrequency of those like me

Not just brown and dark of skin

    It's African Americans, I seek

When traveling domestic shores

    Or foreign and distant lands

Variations of brown are viewed

    But few of Negro[45] strands

    Where are my people?

Sad to say, cannot deny

En masse places we don't go

Converging in cities east, north, and south

We gravitate and grow

Concentrated urbanites

Finding comfort in same

Hesitant to break new ground

Unsure of what can be gained

Going forth, I will welcome

Opportunities to meet and greet

Total strangers of my color

And, those not looking like me

Acknowledging seven continents

With ancestral presence in all

Evidenced by tan, brown, and black

Inscribed on ancient walls

So, when next I ponder

The question I've wondered

I'll know the answer is "clear"

To "Where are my people?"

I will know...

My people are far and near

YOU AIN'T SEEN NOTHING YET!

HOPE and CHANGE

    Promised

HOPE and CHANGE

    Bestowed

Many complained

    Saying, "Not enough!"

    Desiring so much more

Forgetting

    Office attained was not

    President of black Americans

    But, President of the United States of America

    "Of the people, for the people, all the people"

This "Native Son"[46]

    Questioned by birthers[47]

Told us, in 2008

    "Yes, We Can"[48] and yes, he did!

With confidence and intelligence

Establishment did not wish to attach

To those of his ilk[49]

And, not behind, but with, this great man

His equal

A woman of confidence, intelligence

Integrity and family-first values

Not a trophy wife

But a woman accomplished

A woman admired

A woman of strength in character

A woman of strength in mind

A woman capable of standing on her own

His "Wealth of Self"[50]

Confounds those unaccustomed

To men of color with integrity

Men of color with family-first values

Men of color who admonish those

Disrespectful of their family

Not that there are few men of color

Like this man of color

But, those unaccustomed

Choose to remain blind to what is before them

Refusing to acknowledge a black family unit

Of upstanding father

Protective mother

Respected elder, and

Disciplined youth

Exemplify greatness in America

"Drowning In D'Nile"[51]

    Unaccustomed fail to understand

    This man of color challenged thoughts

That...

    A man of his ilk could command

    A man of his ilk could be respected

    A man of his ilk could remain high

    While those not of his ilk went low

Out of office, no longer limited

    By constraints of the oval

    Those who complained

        "Not enough!"

    Be prepared for CHANGE

What may not have been done while in office

    Will get done out of office

Always "of the people, for the people, all the people"

    This family of Chicago

    This family of grassroots

    This family of integrity

    This family of intelligence

    This family of "firsts"

    Have not forgotten from whence they come

This family will continue to fight

    For HOPE and CHANGE

You ain't seen nothing yet!

Obama out!

APPENDIX A

QUOTES

APPENDIX B

JESSE WILLIAMS was honored Sunday, June 26, 2016, at the BET Awards with the Humanitarian Award. The actor/activist, best known for his role on "Grey's Anatomy," has been a visible part of the Black Lives Matter movement since the 2014 events in Ferguson, Missouri.

Following is Jesse Williams' full speech, which is probably one of the most memorable speeches in award show history.

"Peace, peace. Thank you, Debra. Thank you, BET. Thank you Nate Parker, Harry and Debbie Allen for participating in that [pre-recorded video].

Before we get into it, I just want to say I brought my parents out tonight. I just want to thank them for being here, for teaching me to focus on comprehension over career, that they made sure I learned what the schools were afraid to teach us. And also thank my amazing wife for changing my life.

Now, this award – this is not for me. This is for the real organizers all over the country – the activists, the civil rights attorneys, the struggling parents, the families, the teachers, the students that are realizing that a system built to divide and impoverish and destroy us cannot stand if we do. All right? It's kind of basic mathematics – the more we learn about who we are and how we got here, the more we will mobilize.

Now, this is also, in particular, for the black women, in particular, who have spent their lifetimes dedicated to nurturing everyone before themselves. We can and will do better for you.

Now... what we've been doing is looking at the data and we know that police somehow manage to deescalate, disarm and not kill white people everyday. So what's going to happen is we are going to have equal rights and justice in our own country or we will restructure their function and ours.

Now, [standing ovation]... I got more y'all. Yesterday would have been young Tamir Rice's 14th birthday so I don't want to hear anymore about how far we've come when paid public servants can pull a drive-by on a 12-year-old playing alone in the park in broad daylight, killing him on television and then going home to make a sandwich.

Tell Rekia Boyd how it's so much better to live in 2012 than it is to live in 1612 or 1712. Tell that to Eric Garner. Tell that to Sandra Bland. Tell that to Dorian Hunt.

Now, the thing is though... all of us in here getting money – that alone isn't gonna stop this. Alright... now dedicating our lives, dedicating our lives to getting money, just to give it right back for someone's brand on our body when we spent centuries praying with brands on our bodies, and now we pray to get paid for brands on our bodies. There has been no war that we have not fought and died on the front lines of. There has been no job we haven't done. There is no tax they haven't levied against us – and we've paid all of them. But freedom is somehow always conditional here. "You're free," they keep telling us. But she would have been alive if she hadn't acted so... free.

Now, freedom is always coming in the hereafter, but you know what though, the hereafter is a hustle. We want it now. And let's get a couple things straight, just a little side note – the burden of the brutalized is not to comfort the bystander. That's not our job, alright – stop with all that. If you have a critique for the resistance, for our resistance, then you better have an established record of critique of our oppression. If you have no interest, if you have no interest in equal rights for black people then do not make suggestions to those who do. Sit down.

We've been floating this country on credit for centuries, yo. And, we're done watching and waiting while this invention called whiteness uses and abuses us burying black people out of sight and out of mind while extracting our culture, our dollars, our entertainment like oil – black gold, ghettoizing and demeaning our creations then stealing them, gentrifying our genius and then trying us on like costumes before discarding our bodies like rinds of strange fruit. The thing is though... the thing is that just because we're magic doesn't mean we're not real. Thank you."

APPENDIX C

WEST AFRICAN WISDOM
ADINKRA SYMBOLS & MEANINGS

ADINKRAHENE
"chief of Adinkra symbols"
greatness, charisma,
leadership

AKOBEN
"war horn"
vigilance, wariness

AKOFENA
"sword of war"
courage, valor

AKOKONAN
"the leg of a hen"
mercy, nurturing

AKOMA
"the heart"
patience & tolerance

AKOMA NTOSO
"linked hearts"
understanding, agreement

ANANSE NTONTAN
"spider's web"
wisdom, creativity

ASASE YE DURU
"the Earth has weight"
divinity of Mother Earth

AYA
"fern"
endurance,
resourcefulness

BESE SAKA
"sack of cola nuts"
affluence, abundance,
unity

BI NKA BI
"no one should bite the
other"
peace, harmony

**BOA ME NA ME
MMOA WO**
"help me and let me help
you"
cooperation,
interdependence

DAME-DAME
"name of a board game"
intelligence, ingenuity

DENKYEM
"crocodile"
adaptability

DUAFE
"wooden comb"
beauty, hygiene, feminine
qualities

DWENNIMMEN
"ram's horns"
humility and strength

EBAN
"fence"
love, safety, security

EPA
"handcuffs"
law, justice, slavery

ESE NE TEKREMA
"the teeth and the tongue"
friendship,
interdependence

FAWOHODIE
"independence"
independence, freedom,
emancipation

FIHANKRA
"house, compound"
security, safety

FOFO
"a yellow-flowered plant"
jealousy, envy

FUNTUNFUNEFU DENKYEMFUNEFU
"siamese crocodiles"
democracy, unity in diversity

GYE NYAME
"except for God"
supremacy of God

HWEMUDUA
"measuring stick"
examination, quality control

HYE WONHYE
"that which cannot be burnt"
imperishability, endurance

KETE PA
"good bed"
good marriage

KINTINKANTAN
"puffed up extravagance"
arrogance, extravagance

KWATAKYE ATIKO
"hairstyle of Kwatakye, a war hero"
bravery, valor

MATE MASIE
"what I hear, I keep"
wisdom, knowledge, prudence

ME WARE WO
"I shall marry you"
commitment, perseverance

MFRAMADAN
"wind-resistant house"
fortitude, preparedness

MMERE DANE
"time changes"
change, life's dynamics

MMUSUYIDEE
"that which removes ill luck"
good fortune, sanctity

MPATAPO
"knot of reconciliation"
peacemaking, reconciliation

MPUANNUM
"five tufts" (of hair)
priestly office, loyalty, adroitness

NEA ONNIM NO SUA A. OHU
"he who does not know can know from learning"
knowledge, life-long education

NEA OPE SE OBEDI HENE
"he who wants to be king"
service , leadership

NKONSONKONSON
"chain links"
unity, human relations

NYAME DUA
"tree of god"
God's protection and presence

NKYIMU
the crossed divisions made on adinkra cloth before printing
skillfulness, precision

NKYINKYIM
"twistings"
initiative, dynamism, versatility

NSAA
"type of hand-woven cloth"
excellence, genuineness, authenticity

NSOROMMA
"child of the heavens"
guardianship

NYAME BIRIBI WO SORO
"God is in the heavens"
hope

NYAME NNWU NA MAWU
"God never dies, therefore I cannot die"
life after death

NYAME NTI
"by God's grace"
faith & trust in God

NYAME YE OHENE
"God is King"
majesty and supremacy of God

NYANSAPO
"wisdom knot"
wisdom, ingenuity, intelligence & patience

ODO NNYEW FIE KWAN
"love never loses its way home"
power of love

OKODEE MMOWERE
"talons of the eagle"
bravery, strength

ONYANKOPON ADOM NTI BIRIBIARA BEYE YIE
"by God's grace, all will be well"
hope, providence, faith

OSRAM NE NSOROMMA
"the moon and the star"
love, faithfulness, harmony

OWO FORO ADOBE
"snake climbing the raffia tree"
steadfastness, prudence, diligence

OWUO ATWEDEE
"the ladder of death"
mortality

PEMPAMSIE
"sew in readiness"
readiness, steadfastness

SANKOFA
"return and get it"
learn from the past

SANKOFA
"return and get it"
learn from the past
(alternate version)

SESA WO SUBAN
"I change or transform my life"
transformation

TAMPO BEBRE
"the enemy will stew in his own juice"
jealousy

WAWA ABA
"seed of the wawa tree"
hardiness, toughness, perseverance

WOFORO DUA PA A
"when you climb a good tree"
support, cooperation

WO NSA DA MU A
"if your hands are in the dish"
democracy, pluralism

YOUR WORDS ABOUT MY WORDS

ABOUT THE AUTHOR

"We shall not be denied our prominence; we shall not be denied our contributions; we shall not be denied our respect; and, we shall not be denied our equality. We are citizens of the first-class."

Y.B. Taylor

Y.B. Taylor was born in Richmond, Virginia, a former seat of the Confederacy, the same year as the landmark decision of *Brown v. Board of Education* (1954). Current events, history, and life experiences of being born and raised in a segregated community, as well as her introduction to integration through education and employment are the inspirations for her poetry.

Y.B. Taylor was one of six "Negro" students to integrate Albert H. Hill Junior High in 1966 and Huguenot High School's first African American varsity cheerleader and homecoming queen. A direct result of her being homecoming queen was her inclusion in the Miss Chesterfield Beauty Pageant, becoming one of the two firsts black contestants in the history of the pageant. She has experienced being the proverbial "only fly in the ointment" in corporate settings and has had her ethnicity questioned for no other reason than the position she held or the manner in which she carried herself and spoke.

Y.B. Taylor resides in Henrico, Virginia, with her husband. They are extremely proud parents of two married and accomplished daughters. There are no bloodline grandchildren at the time of this publication, however, there is a "grand" in Chester, Virginia; a grand-dog in Brooklyn, New York; and, two grand-cats in Glen Burnie, Maryland.

Twitter: @YB_Taylor   ✉ y.b.taylo@yolandabtaylorwrites.com

🇫 @Y.B.TaylorWrites

ENDNOTES

---

[1] Maternal grandfather passed in 1939.

[2] Philando Castile, in Falcon Heights, Minnesota, 10-days shy of his 33rd birthday; Alton Sterling, 37, in Baton Rouge, Louisiana

[3] The assailant, Micah Johnson, who revenged killed the officers had been deemed *unstable*, banned, and kicked out of the Army.

[4] The usage of *ain't* is a subject of controversy in English. *Ain't* is commonly used by speakers in oral or informal settings, especially in certain regions and dialects. Its usage is highly stigmatized, and it has been used as a marker of low socio-economic or regional status or education level. Its use is considered non-standard by dictionaries and style guides except when used for rhetorical effect, and it is rarely found in formal written works.

[5] Malia and Sasha Obama, daughters of first African American President of the United States (POTUS), Barack Obama, and First Lady of the United States (FLOTUS), Michelle Obama.

[6] The urban dictionary defines **shade** as acting in a casual or disrespectful manner towards someone/"dissing" or disrespecting a friend; throwing shade, acting kind of shady

[7] San Francisco 49ers quarterback Colin Kaepernick willingly immersed himself into controversy by refusing to stand for playing of the national anthem in protest of what he deems are wrongdoings against African Americans and minorities in the United States.

[8] Words attributed to Malcolm X's Speech at the Founding Rally of the Organization of Afro-American Unity on June 28,1964, the last year of his life. "We want freedom **by any means necessary**. We want justice **by any means necessary**. We want equality **by any means necessary**. We don't feel that in 1964, ..."

[9] One of author's favorite quotes – *"Excuses are tools of incompetence, built on monuments of nothingness and those who practice in their use are seldom capable of anything else."* -- Anonymous

[10] Four-time Olympian and United States swimmer Ryan Lochte, age 32, told NBC's Matt Lauer it was his fault that a fabricated story about a robbery caused an international Olympics scandal. (2016 Olympics in Rio)

[11] California judge gives Brock Turner, a former Stanford University swimmer, a six-month jail sentence for sexually assaulting an unconscious woman. Turner's father initially dismissed his son's crime as "20 minutes of action."

[12] Tamir Rice, age 12, was shot and killed when two police officers responded to a police dispatch call "of a male black sitting on a swing and pointing a gun at people" in a city park.

[13] Cameron Tillman, age 14, was fatally shot, by police, upon responding to a knock on the door of a house, which had been empty for about two years, and neighbors say local kids, with the knowledge of the owner, had been using as an afterschool hangout.

[14] James Means, 15, was shot and killed by William Pulliam in Charleston, West Virginia, after an accidental bump outside a Dollar General store. A police detective quoted Pulliam as saying, "The way I look at it, that's another piece of trash off the street."

[15] Laquan McDonald, age 17, was fatally shot 16 times as he walked in the street with a knife.

[16] Horoscope sun sign, **Virgo, August 20 – September 20.** Jada Pinkett Smith's day of birth, **September 18**; Beyonce (Knowle's) day of birth, **September 4.**

[17] Invoking Rev. Martin Luther King's legacy on his birthday [January 15, 2016], filmmaker Spike Lee and actress Jada Pinkett Smith announce they will boycott the Oscars ceremony [February 28, 2016]. In separate messages, both criticized the Academy Awards for a lack of diversity among nominees. The Oscars drew criticism after an all-white slate of major nominees was announced for the second year in a row.

[18] Beyonce's release of "Formation" video and performance at Super Bowl 50 ignited controversy. The video advocated for African American lives. The video addresses police brutality, Hurricane Katrina and black power, among other black community struggles.

[19] Translates as "covering your back," six comes from being behind a person (six o' clock position). So, "watch my six" is "cover me from behind." (Urban Dictionary)

[20] **Brown Paper Bag Test,** an example of an exclusionary practice, was a discriminatory act that was based on skin color and acceptance. The brown paper bag was used as a measurement to determine whether or not an individual could receive access to certain privileges; individuals were given preference if having a skin tone lighter than a brown paper bag.

[21] A palindrome poem (or mirror poem) uses the same words in the first half of the poem as the second half; reverses the order for the second half; and, uses a word in the middle as a bridge from the first half to the second half of the poem. In this instance, the poet has used four lines rather than one word as the bridge between the first and second halves of the poem.

[22] Following the lead of Colin Kaepernick of the San Francisco 49ers, several athletes during 2016 sports season, expressed their concerns about a lot of issues in this country. Many expressed their sentiments about racial inequality, oppression, and injustice by sitting or taking a knee during the traditional playing of the National Anthem before games.

[23] Olympic sprinters Tommie Smith and John Carlos held up their fists in a black power salute during a medals ceremony at the 1968 Olympic games in Mexico City.

[24] Exhibition examined realities of life under segregation in 1950s America, as seen through lens of groundbreaking photographer Gordon Parks (1912–2006). As first African American photographer hired full time by *Life* magazine, Parks was frequently given assignments involving social issues affecting black America. In 1950, one such project took him back to his hometown in Kansas for a photo essay he planned to call "Back to Fort Scott."

[25] The gelatin silver process was introduced at the end of the 19th century and dominated black-and-white photography in the 20th century. The paper or film used to make gelatin silver prints and negatives is coated with an emulsion that contains gelatin and silver salts.

[26] "Give me your tired, your poor, Your huddled masses yearning to breathe free, The wretched refuse of your teeming shore. Send these, the homeless, tempest-

tossed to me, I lift my lamp beside the golden door!" The **Statue of Liberty**-Ellis Island Foundation, Inc.

[27] In 1838 and 1839, as part of Andrew Jackson's Indian removal policy, the Cherokee nation was forced to give up its lands east of the Mississippi River and to migrate to an area in present-day Oklahoma. The Cherokee people called this journey the "**Trail of Tears**," because of its devastating effects.

[28] Pronounced **chuh-kruhm**, yoga term meaning 'energy center'

[29] Pronounced **ooo-jay-ee**, yoga term for very calming breathing technique; slightly constrict back of throat during inhalation and exhalation giving breath audible, oceanic sounding quality.

[30] Pronounced **vihn-yah-sah**, literally means to place in a special way; refers to linking of movement with breath through series of postures.

[31] Pronounced **sah-vah-sahnah**, yoga term for corpse pose, the final posture in most classes

[32] Pronounced **nah-mah-stay**, yoga term meaning "I bow to you."

[33] From **Voices from the Days of Slavery: Stories, Songs and Memories** for Library of Congress

[34] Use of **we** and **us** is purposeful for inclusion of, but not limited to minorities, women, forward-thinkers, LGBT+ community, immigrants, Muslims, etc.

[35] After election of 45th President, Trump supporters verbally and physically assault citizens not conforming to their "ideal" American.

[36] Smithsonian Institute added to its footprint on the National Mall in Washington, D.C., with the grand opening of the National Museum of African American History and Culture (NMAAHC), Saturday, September 24, 2016

[37] Vivien Thomas, African American surgical technician who developed the procedures used to treat blue baby syndrome in 1940s; served as supervisor of surgical laboratories at Johns Hopkins for 35 years. Without education pass high school, was awarded honorary doctorate and named an instructor of surgery in 1976. Television film based on his life, *Something the Lord Made*.

[38] Simone Manuel, freestyle swimmer, wins two gold and two silver medals at 2016 Rio Olympics.

[39] Barack Hussein Obama becomes 44th U.S. President and first African American POTUS; serves two terms, 2008-2012 and 2012-2016

[40] An African Zulu greeting that means "I see you." It has a long oral history and it means more than the traditional "hello." It says, "I see your personality. I see your humanity. I see your dignity and respect." In the African village context, where everyone knows one another, it's an exceedingly powerful representation of understanding.

[41] Originally established in the Village of Mitchelville, in 1862, there were 120 members that made up the first congregation, all of whom were considered "contrabands."

[42] Hannibal is often regarded as one of the greatest military strategists in history and one of the greatest generals of antiquity. Military historian Theodore Ayrault Dodge called Hannibal the "father of strategy", because his greatest enemy, Rome, came to adopt elements of his military tactics in its own strategic arsenal. This praise earned him a strong reputation in the modern world; he was regarded as a great strategist by Napoleon and others.

[43] Before it was the Arc de Triomphe, the space was almost dedicated to a giant elephant. Napoleon planned first to place at the far end of the Champs-Élysées, a statue of an elephant in order to recall and honor the ancient conqueror Hannibal but then decided on a massive Arc de Triomphe in order to celebrate his own victories. (NOTE: Construction of the elephant's trunk would have been a architectural nightmare.)

[44] Crème fraîche, a soured cream containing 10–45% butterfat and having a pH of around 4.5, soured with bacterial culture, but less sour than United States-style sour cream, has a lower viscosity and higher fat content.

[45] "The Negro was invented in America." – quote by novelist, screenwriter, and editor John Oliver Killens (1916-1987).

[46] Title of poem found in Y.B. Taylor's, "What I Know…Poems of Life" ©2009

[47] A person who doubts the legitimacy of Barack Obama's presidency because of a conspiracy theory that Obama was not a natural-born United States citizen.

[48] Title of poem found in Y.B. Taylor's "What I Know…Poems of Life" ©2009

[49] A type of people or things similar to those already referred to.

[50] Title of poem found in Y.B. Taylor's "Journeys of Freedom" ©2011

[51] Title of poem found in Y.B. Taylor's "Keeping It Real! A Book of Poetry and No Excuses" ©2015

Made in the USA
Middletown, DE
31 October 2020